Clip-Art Cartoons FOR CHURCHES

Your newsletter just got 180 times funnier!

(And more people are reading it, too!)

SPICE UP YOUR...

- handouts • letterhead • overhead transparencies
- church bulletins • fliers • business cards • calendars
- reports • invitations • and other printed pieces

you create—with these 180+ hilarious cartoons!

Photocopy the cartoon that fits your theme, pop it into place, and presto—you've as much as *doubled* the number of people who will read what you've written!

And it's *legal!* You have full permission to use these side-splitters in any non-profit church publication you want...anyplace...anywhere...any time!

Each cartoon is reproduced in the sizes you're most likely to use...and cartoons cover a wide range of themes:

- Church life
- Youth group
- Sermons
- Volunteers...
- Sunday school
- School life
- Church events

...AND MORE!

Put a half-dozen of the country's top cartoonists to work for you now...and increase the imp everything you distribute!

Group®
Printed in the U.S.A.

© 1994 James Cook

ISBN 1-55945-791-0

9 781559 457910

05 98/ 1
$22.50

YOUTH MINISTRY/
CHURCH SUPPLIES

Carleton U.C.
1998.

Clip-Art
Cartoons
FOR CHURCHES

Group®
Loveland, Colorado

NOTE

The price of this product includes the right for you to make copies of the art included in it for nonprofit use only, such as in church newsletters, bulletins, correspondence, brochures, or other nonprofit publications. If such use involves 1,000 copies or more, each copy must cite the title and publisher of this book as follows: "From Clip-Art Cartoons for Churches, Group Publishing, Inc. Used by permission." All other uses require prior written permission from the publisher.

CREDITS
Editor: Mike Nappa
Senior Editor: Paul Woods
Creative Products Director: Joani Schultz
Copy Editor: Candace McMahan
Art Director: Lisa Smith
Cover Art Director: Liz Howe
Designers: Helen Lannis and Lisa Smith
Computer Graphic Artist: Randy Kady
Illustrators: James Cook, John Duckworth, Randy Glasbergen, Doug Hall, John McPherson, Rob Portlock, and Ron Wheeler
Production Manager: Gingar Kunkel

ISBN 1-55945-791-0
10 9 8 7 6 5 4 3 2   04 03 02 01 00 99 98 97
Printed in the United States of America.

CONTENTS

"You should get a halo! That would look awesome!"

"OOOO! ... I REALLY FELT _CONVICTED_ BY YOUR SERMON TODAY, CHAPLAIN."

"...and 600,000 flat breads to go."

INTRODUCTION

Hee hee hee . . . Oh, excuse me. I *(ha-ha)* didn't realize you were reading this introduction already. *(Snicker.)* Sorry, but I've been scanning through the contents of the book *(ho ho ho)*, and I can't stop laughing. *(Ha ha ha—Naugahyde! Ha ha!)* OK, OK. Let me set the cartoons down so I can concentrate . . . Now, let's see *(whooo)* . . .

Oh, yes! Welcome to the book you've been waiting years for—*Clip-Art Cartoons for Churches.* You hold in your hand a treasury of over 180 cartoons about the Christian life that'll bring giggles and smiles to the faces of all who read them.

And the best part is: You can photocopy them legally!

You no longer have to slink around, hoping the photocopy police won't discover that you secretly sneaked a McPherson cartoon into your church newsletter. Do you like Rob Portlock's humor on page 69? Fine, photocopy the cartoon and include it in a letter to a friend!

As a matter of fact, seven of today's best Christian cartoonists have given you their blessings to share their work in your nonprofit publications such as church newsletters, bulletins, correspondence, brochures, classroom handouts, overhead transparencies, and fliers. (You can also simply make a copy for your bulletin board or refrigerator!)

In this photocopiable cartoon collection, you'll find humorous glimpses of church life through light-hearted looks at sermons, offerings, choirs, office life, and church facilities. You'll also get a laugh at Sunday school's expense by reading funny interpretations of Bible stories and humorous characterizations of teachers, students, and classrooms. There are quirky cartoons about youth groups and school life, church events, volunteers, sports, visitors, outreach, the clergy, and more.

I could go on and on, but I really want you to read the cartoons in this book. So maybe it's best to wrap up this introduction. Besides, I need to copy a cartoon on page 77. I want to use it in my next newsletter.

Enjoy!

—Mike Nappa, Editor

"Remember, this is a *church* picnic—so always say 'amen' after you burp!"

UPON VISITING HIS FORMER CHURCH JUST THREE MONTHS AFTER LEAVING, PASTOR BRUCE FERNLOCK DISCOVERS THAT HIS IMPACT THERE WASN'T NEARLY AS PROFOUND AS HE HAD THOUGHT.

"They have a peculiar way of greeting first-time visitors."

THE HOTTER THE WEATHER BECAME, THE LESS PEOPLE
LIKED THE NEW NAUGAHYDE PEW CUSHIONS.

THE HOTTER THE WEATHER BECAME, THE LESS PEOPLE
LIKED THE NEW NAUGAHYDE PEW CUSHIONS.

THE HOTTER THE WEATHER BECAME, THE LESS PEOPLE
LIKED THE NEW NAUGAHYDE PEW CUSHIONS.

ATTEMPTS TO MAKE THE CHURCH NEWSLETTER
MORE EXCITING TO READ WERE GETTING OUT OF HAND.

ATTEMPTS TO MAKE THE CHURCH NEWSLETTER
MORE EXCITING TO READ WERE GETTING OUT OF HAND.

ATTEMPTS TO MAKE THE CHURCH NEWSLETTER
MORE EXCITING TO READ WERE GETTING OUT OF HAND.

"TV's influence in our lives is my sermon topic today."

"TV's influence in our lives is my sermon topic today."

"TV's influence in our lives is my sermon topic today."

"You should get a halo! That would look awesome!"

"You should get a halo! That would look awesome!"

"You should get a halo! That would look awesome!"

ALTHOUGH THE NEW GRADUATION PROCESS AT BURNSVILLE HIGH WAS FASTER, IT DIDN'T QUITE HAVE THE GLAMOUR OF THE TRADITIONAL GRADUATION CEREMONY.

ALTHOUGH THE NEW GRADUATION PROCESS AT BURNSVILLE HIGH WAS FASTER, IT DIDN'T QUITE HAVE THE GLAMOUR OF THE TRADITIONAL GRADUATION CEREMONY.

VISITORS TO PINE POINT CHURCH COULD SENSE A PROBLEM WITH CLIQUES AMONG THE CONGREGATION, SUBTLE THOUGH IT WAS.

ALTHOUGH THE NEW GRADUATION PROCESS AT BURNSVILLE HIGH WAS FASTER, IT DIDN'T QUITE HAVE THE GLAMOUR OF THE TRADITIONAL GRADUATION CEREMONY.

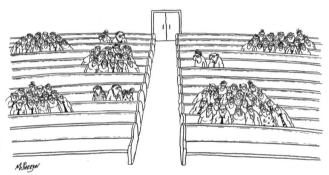

VISITORS TO PINE POINT CHURCH COULD SENSE A PROBLEM WITH CLIQUES AMONG THE CONGREGATION, SUBTLE THOUGH IT WAS.

VISITORS TO PINE POINT CHURCH COULD SENSE A PROBLEM WITH CLIQUES AMONG THE CONGREGATION, SUBTLE THOUGH IT WAS.

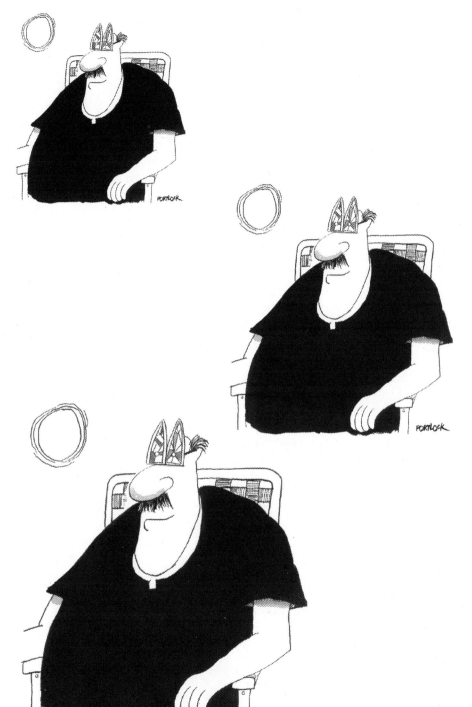

"THE COFFEE MAKER IS BROKEN."

"THE COFFEE MAKER IS BROKEN."

"THE COFFEE MAKER IS BROKEN."

James Cook

Few suspected the true
reason for the concise nature of
Pastor Brown's sermon.

James Cook

Few suspected the true
reason for the concise nature of
Pastor Brown's sermon.

James Cook

Few suspected the true
reason for the concise nature of
Pastor Brown's sermon.

"I never thought promising to shorten my
sermon would affect the offering."

"I never thought promising to shorten my
sermon would affect the offering."

"I never thought promising to shorten my
sermon would affect the offering."

"MANY THANKS TO THE LADIES QUILTING CLUB FOR PROVIDING US WITH THESE LOVELY NEW CHOIR ROBES."

"MANY THANKS TO THE LADIES QUILTING CLUB FOR PROVIDING US WITH THESE LOVELY NEW CHOIR ROBES."

"MANY THANKS TO THE LADIES QUILTING CLUB FOR PROVIDING US WITH THESE LOVELY NEW CHOIR ROBES."

"We'd like to thank the choir for that rousing number."

"We'd like to thank the choir for that rousing number."

"We'd like to thank the choir for that rousing number."

James Cook

YOUTH PASTOR DAN CLYDELL FACES THE TOUGHEST
SEARCH COMMITTEE OF HIS NINE-YEAR CAREER.

YOU'RE ON A YOUTH RETREAT WHEN A KID PUTS A MILDLY
POISONOUS SNAKE DOWN YOUR SHIRT. DO YOU
A. ASSIGN HIM 24 HOURS OF LATRINE DUTY,
B. SEND HIM HOME AND RECOMMEND HARSH DISCIPLINE, OR
C. LAUGH IT OFF AS JUST A HARMLESS PRANK?

YOUTH PASTOR DAN CLYDELL FACES THE TOUGHEST
SEARCH COMMITTEE OF HIS NINE-YEAR CAREER.

James Cook

Although grateful for healing and eager to follow Jesus, Bud hesitates
to give up his only worldly possession.

Although grateful for healing and eager to follow Jesus, Bud hesitates
to give up his only worldly possession.

THE NEW, CONVERGING CONFERENCE ROOM WALLS HELPED TO
KEEP MEETINGS SHORT AND TO THE POINT.

THE NEW, CONVERGING CONFERENCE ROOM WALLS HELPED TO
KEEP MEETINGS SHORT AND TO THE POINT.

THE NEW, CONVERGING CONFERENCE ROOM WALLS HELPED TO
KEEP MEETINGS SHORT AND TO THE POINT.

Verna feared that the government's new potluck regulations
would have a chilling effect on consumption of her
chicken-skin casserole.

Verna feared that the government's new potluck regulations
would have a chilling effect on consumption of her
chicken-skin casserole.

Verna feared that the government's new potluck regulations
would have a chilling effect on consumption of her
chicken-skin casserole.

James Cook

"...and 600,000 flat breads to go."

James Cook

" "...and 600,000 flat breads to go. "

James Cook

" "...and 600,000 flat breads to go. "

"Honey, wake up! You're preaching in your sleep again."

"Honey, wake up! You're preaching in your sleep again."

"Honey, wake up! You're preaching in your sleep again."

AFTER MONTHS OF PLANNING, MANAGEMENT REVEALS THE NEW REORGANIZATION PLAN.

AFTER MONTHS OF PLANNING, MANAGEMENT REVEALS THE NEW REORGANIZATION PLAN.

"That was a lovely hymn, choir, but could you do it an octave lower next time?"

"That was a lovely hymn, choir, but could you do it an octave lower next time?"

AFTER MONTHS OF PLANNING, MANAGEMENT REVEALS THE NEW REORGANIZATION PLAN.

"That was a lovely hymn, choir, but could you do it an octave lower next time?"

"I want to withdraw my tithes from the last 28 years."

"I want to withdraw my tithes from the last 28 years."

"I want to withdraw my tithes from the last 28 years."

"I'D LIKE TO OFFER A SPECIAL THANKS TO ALL OF YOU FOR COMING THROUGH IN THE CLUTCH TO MAKE THIS YEAR'S CLOTHING DRIVE A BIG SUCCESS."

"I'D LIKE TO OFFER A SPECIAL THANKS TO ALL OF YOU FOR COMING THROUGH IN THE CLUTCH TO MAKE THIS YEAR'S CLOTHING DRIVE A BIG SUCCESS."

"I'D LIKE TO OFFER A SPECIAL THANKS TO ALL OF YOU FOR COMING THROUGH IN THE CLUTCH TO MAKE THIS YEAR'S CLOTHING DRIVE A BIG SUCCESS."

PEOPLE WERE STARTING TO THINK THAT HOME ECONOMICS TEACHER SELMA LAVITZ WASN'T THE BEST CHOICE TO FILL THE ASSISTANT COACHING POSITION.

PEOPLE WERE STARTING TO THINK THAT HOME ECONOMICS TEACHER SELMA LAVITZ WASN'T THE BEST CHOICE TO FILL THE ASSISTANT COACHING POSITION.

PEOPLE WERE STARTING TO THINK THAT HOME ECONOMICS TEACHER SELMA LAVITZ WASN'T THE BEST CHOICE TO FILL THE ASSISTANT COACHING POSITION.

"The church treasurer says we can write off our trip to Orlando."

"The church treasurer says we can write off our trip to Orlando."

"The church treasurer says we can write off our trip to Orlando."

THE LATEST IN THE EVER-EXPANDING ARRAY OF
CHRISTIAN PRODUCTS.

THE LATEST IN THE EVER-EXPANDING ARRAY OF
CHRISTIAN PRODUCTS.

THE LATEST IN THE EVER-EXPANDING ARRAY OF
CHRISTIAN PRODUCTS.

"Do you bow your head often?"

"Do you bow your head often?"

"Do you bow your head often?"

"And about their breath..."

James Cook

"And about their breath..."

James Cook

"And about their breath..."

James Cook

"IT SAYS ON YOUR RÉSUMÉ THAT YOU CAN TYPE 260 WORDS PER MINUTE. NO OFFENSE, MRS. BALLAS, BUT I FIND THAT PRETTY HARD TO BELIEVE."

"IT SAYS ON YOUR RÉSUMÉ THAT YOU CAN TYPE 260 WORDS PER MINUTE. NO OFFENSE, MRS. BALLAS, BUT I FIND THAT PRETTY HARD TO BELIEVE."

"IT SAYS ON YOUR RÉSUMÉ THAT YOU CAN TYPE 260 WORDS PER MINUTE. NO OFFENSE, MRS. BALLAS, BUT I FIND THAT PRETTY HARD TO BELIEVE."

"No, smarty. We don't have smoke detectors here."

"No, smarty. We don't have smoke detectors here."

"No, smarty. We don't have smoke detectors here."

"DIRECT THE YOUTH CHOIR? UH . . . SURE, NO PROBLEM.
WHAT? NO, GLAD TO DO IT! REALLY."

"DIRECT THE YOUTH CHOIR? UH . . . SURE, NO PROBLEM.
WHAT? NO, GLAD TO DO IT! REALLY."

"DIRECT THE YOUTH CHOIR? UH . . . SURE, NO PROBLEM.
WHAT? NO, GLAD TO DO IT! REALLY."

"How could God rest on the seventh day
if TV and recliners weren't created yet?"

"How could God rest on the seventh day
if TV and recliners weren't created yet?"

"How could God rest on the seventh day
if TV and recliners weren't created yet?"

"Our organist died 12 years ago, but she left us her soundtrack."

"Our organist died 12 years ago, but she left us her soundtrack."

"Our organist died 12 years ago, but she left us her soundtrack."

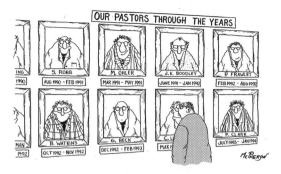

NEWLY HIRED PASTOR MILTON FELDSPAR WAS STARTING TO
WONDER WHAT HE'D GOTTEN HIMSELF INTO.

NEWLY HIRED PASTOR MILTON FELDSPAR WAS STARTING TO
WONDER WHAT HE'D GOTTEN HIMSELF INTO.

"THIS NEW CHOIR DIRECTOR CERTAINLY HAS SPUNK!"

"THIS NEW CHOIR DIRECTOR CERTAINLY HAS SPUNK!"

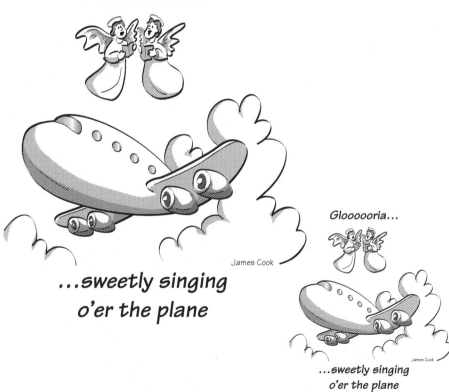

Glooooooria...

...sweetly singing
o'er the plane

James Cook

Glooooooria...

...sweetly singing
o'er the plane

James Cook

THE PASTORAL SELECTION COMMITTEE AT MILL VALLEY CHURCH WAS KNOWN FOR ITS IMPERSONAL INTERVIEWING PROCESS.

THE PASTORAL SELECTION COMMITTEE AT MILL VALLEY CHURCH WAS KNOWN FOR ITS IMPERSONAL INTERVIEWING PROCESS.

THE PASTORAL SELECTION COMMITTEE AT MILL VALLEY CHURCH WAS KNOWN FOR ITS IMPERSONAL INTERVIEWING PROCESS.

"I'VE GOT A FEELING THIS ISN'T GOING TO DO WONDERS FOR OUR LAB GRADES."

"I'VE GOT A FEELING THIS ISN'T GOING TO DO WONDERS FOR OUR LAB GRADES."

"I'VE GOT A FEELING THIS ISN'T GOING TO DO WONDERS FOR OUR LAB GRADES."

"HAVE I BEEN IGNORING YOU, DEAR, OR DID
YOU JUST FIND ANOTHER DANDY COUPON?"

"HAVE I BEEN IGNORING YOU, DEAR, OR DID
YOU JUST FIND ANOTHER DANDY COUPON?"

"HAVE I BEEN IGNORING YOU, DEAR, OR DID
YOU JUST FIND ANOTHER DANDY COUPON?"

"Pastor Jim recommended this video! It's the *Spirit of Steel* workout!"

"Pastor Jim recommended this video! It's the *Spirit of Steel* workout!"

"Pastor Jim recommended this video! It's the *Spirit of Steel* workout!"

SCANDAL ROCKED THE MAPLE VALLEY CHURCH WHEN IT WAS DISCOVERED THAT THE CHOIR HAD BEEN LIP-SYNCING FOR THE LAST SIX YEARS.

SCANDAL ROCKED THE MAPLE VALLEY CHURCH WHEN IT WAS DISCOVERED THAT THE CHOIR HAD BEEN LIP-SYNCING FOR THE LAST SIX YEARS.

SCANDAL ROCKED THE MAPLE VALLEY CHURCH WHEN IT WAS DISCOVERED THAT THE CHOIR HAD BEEN LIP-SYNCING FOR THE LAST SIX YEARS.

GREAT MOMENTS IN CHURCH HISTORY:
THE FIRST BUILDING PROGRAM IS LAUNCHED WHEN THE FIRST-CENTURY CHRISTIANS DECIDE THE UPPER ROOM NEEDED A NEW WING.

GREAT MOMENTS IN CHURCH HISTORY:
THE FIRST BUILDING PROGRAM IS LAUNCHED WHEN THE FIRST-CENTURY CHRISTIANS DECIDE THE UPPER ROOM NEEDED A NEW WING.

GREAT MOMENTS IN CHURCH HISTORY:
THE FIRST BUILDING PROGRAM IS LAUNCHED WHEN THE FIRST-CENTURY CHRISTIANS DECIDE THE UPPER ROOM NEEDED A NEW WING.

"YEAH, I KNOW. IT'S A RIDICULOUS COMMITTEE. BUT WE WANTED TO FIND SOME WAY TO GET MORE MEN USED TO THE IDEA OF SERVING ON COMMITTEES."

"YEAH, I KNOW. IT'S A RIDICULOUS COMMITTEE. BUT WE WANTED TO FIND SOME WAY TO GET MORE MEN USED TO THE IDEA OF SERVING ON COMMITTEES."

"YEAH, I KNOW. IT'S A RIDICULOUS COMMITTEE. BUT WE WANTED TO FIND SOME WAY TO GET MORE MEN USED TO THE IDEA OF SERVING ON COMMITTEES."

ALTHOUGH INTENDED TO BOOST THE TEAM'S MORALE, COACH FINKLEY'S REWARD SYSTEM FOR MAKING A BASKET ACTUALLY HAD THE REVERSE EFFECT.

ALTHOUGH INTENDED TO BOOST THE TEAM'S MORALE, COACH FINKLEY'S REWARD SYSTEM FOR MAKING A BASKET ACTUALLY HAD THE REVERSE EFFECT.

ALTHOUGH INTENDED TO BOOST THE TEAMS MORALE, COACH FINKLEY'S REWARD SYSTEM FOR MAKING A BASKET ACTUALLY HAD THE REVERSE EFFECT.

"In keeping with current federal food-labeling laws, the complete protein, carbohydrate, and fat content of this morning's Communion may be found on page 3 of your bulletins."

"In keeping with current federal food-labeling laws, the complete protein, carbohydrate, and fat content of this morning's Communion may be found on page 3 of your bulletins."

"In keeping with current federal food-labeling laws, the complete protein, carbohydrate, and fat content of this morning's Communion may be found on page 3 of your bulletins."

"The planning committee plans to meet Tuesday evening
to plan a meeting to make plans for planning the next planning session."

"The planning committee plans to meet Tuesday evening
to plan a meeting to make plans for planning the next planning session."

"The planning committee plans to meet Tuesday evening
to plan a meeting to make plans for planning the next planning session."

"I'd know the back of those heads anywhere.
We sit behind them at church."

"I'd know the back of those heads anywhere.
We sit behind them at church."

"I'd know the back of those heads anywhere.
We sit behind them at church."

REVEREND SPILLMAN'S IDEA OF COMMUNITY INVOLVEMENT WAS VASTLY DIFFERENT FROM THAT OF THE CHURCH BOARD.

REVEREND SPILLMAN'S IDEA OF COMMUNITY INVOLVEMENT WAS VASTLY DIFFERENT FROM THAT OF THE CHURCH BOARD.

REVEREND SPILLMAN'S IDEA OF COMMUNITY INVOLVEMENT WAS VASTLY DIFFERENT FROM THAT OF THE CHURCH BOARD.

"TODAY'S COLLECTION WILL GO TOWARD THE PURCHASE OF A NEW ROOF."

"TODAY'S COLLECTION WILL GO TOWARD THE PURCHASE OF A NEW ROOF."

"TODAY'S COLLECTION WILL GO TOWARD THE PURCHASE OF A NEW ROOF."

CLEARLY, THE NEW ORGANIST WAS NOT GOING TO WORK OUT.

CLEARLY, THE NEW ORGANIST WAS NOT GOING TO WORK OUT.

CLEARLY, THE NEW ORGANIST WAS NOT GOING TO WORK OUT.

James Cook

Daniel in the Lion's Den

Aug 9k

James Cook

Daniel in the Lion's Den

Daniel in the Lion's Den

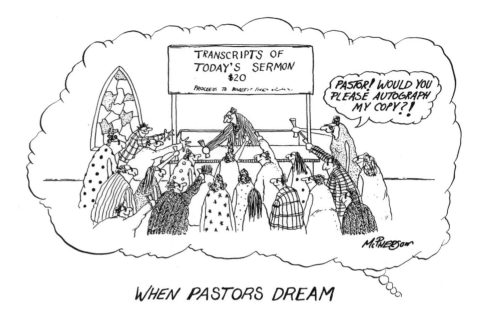

WHEN PASTORS DREAM

WHEN PASTORS DREAM

WHEN PASTORS DREAM

"In church bowling league, we always roll the ball real slooooooow.
That way we have more time to pray for a strike."

"In church bowling league, we always roll the ball real slooooooow.
That way we have more time to pray for a strike."

"In church bowling league, we always roll the ball real slooooooow.
That way we have more time to pray for a strike."

THOUGH A COMPROMISE HAD BEEN MADE, THERE STILL SEEMED
TO BE SOME TENSION BETWEEN PEOPLE WHO WANTED SERVICES
TO BE HELD AT 9:30A.M. AND THOSE WHO WANTED THEM AT 11:00A.M.

THOUGH A COMPROMISE HAD BEEN MADE, THERE STILL SEEMED
TO BE SOME TENSION BETWEEN PEOPLE WHO WANTED SERVICES
TO BE HELD AT 9:30A.M. AND THOSE WHO WANTED THEM AT 11:00A.M.

THOUGH A COMPROMISE HAD BEEN MADE, THERE STILL SEEMED
TO BE SOME TENSION BETWEEN PEOPLE WHO WANTED SERVICES
TO BE HELD AT 9:30A.M. AND THOSE WHO WANTED THEM AT 11:00A.M.

THE SEARCH COMMITTEE RETURNS FROM A SUCCESSFUL OUTING.

THE SEARCH COMMITTEE RETURNS FROM A SUCCESSFUL OUTING.

THE SEARCH COMMITTEE RETURNS FROM A SUCCESSFUL OUTING.

"Unfortunately, you've stumbled into our Seeker-Insensitive Service."

"Unfortunately, you've stumbled into our Seeker-Insensitive Service."

"Unfortunately, you've stumbled into our Seeker-Insensitive Service."

Everyone wondered how the
janitor changed those
light bulbs in the sanctuary,
but he would never tell.

Everyone wondered how the
janitor changed those
light bulbs in the sanctuary,
but he would never tell.

Everyone wondered how the
janitor changed those
light bulbs in the sanctuary,
but he would never tell.

"TO KEEP THE KIDS FROM GETTING OUT?
ARE YOU KIDDING?! WE LOCK IT UP TO KEEP
THE TEACHERS FROM GETTING OUT!"

"TO KEEP THE KIDS FROM GETTING OUT?
ARE YOU KIDDING?! WE LOCK IT UP TO KEEP
THE TEACHERS FROM GETTING OUT!"

"TO KEEP THE KIDS FROM GETTING OUT?
ARE YOU KIDDING?! WE LOCK IT UP TO KEEP
THE TEACHERS FROM GETTING OUT!"

"IT'S PART OF THE COMPANY'S NEW EMPHASIS ON HEALTH AND FITNESS."

"IT'S PART OF THE COMPANY'S NEW EMPHASIS ON HEALTH AND FITNESS."

"IT'S PART OF THE COMPANY'S NEW EMPHASIS ON HEALTH AND FITNESS."

LECTURE
A TEENAGER
ABOUT WHAT'S WRONG
WITH KIDS TODAY!
$2.50

At the youth group fund-raiser,
Andy's booth was a big success.

LECTURE
A TEENAGER
ABOUT WHAT'S WRONG
WITH KIDS TODAY!
$2.50

At the youth group fund-raiser,
Andy's booth was a big success.

LECTURE
A TEENAGER
ABOUT WHAT'S WRONG
WITH KIDS TODAY!
$2.50

At the youth group fund-raiser,
Andy's booth was a big success.

DUE TO THE GREETING PROCESS AT POTTER CREEK CHURCH, FIRST-TIME VISITORS RARELY BECAME SECOND-TIME VISITORS.

DUE TO THE GREETING PROCESS AT POTTER CREEK CHURCH, FIRST-TIME VISITORS RARELY BECAME SECOND-TIME VISITORS.

DUE TO THE GREETING PROCESS AT POTTER CREEK CHURCH, FIRST-TIME VISITORS RARELY BECAME SECOND-TIME VISITORS.

"It's a present from the congregation."

FATHER KNOWS BEST

FATHER KNOWS BEST

"It's a present from the congregation."

"It's a present from the congregation."

"I haven't actually heard God's voice. I just get the feeling he wants me for some purpose."

"I haven't actually heard God's voice. I just get the feeling he wants me for some purpose."

"I thought it might be an appropriate time to give a sermon on anger."

"I thought it might be an appropriate time to give a sermon on anger."

"I thought it might be an appropriate time to give a sermon on anger."

"To meet the ever-growing needs of our congregation, Communion will begin this morning at 11:45. Fat-free Communion will begin at 12:05, high-fiber Communion will begin at 12:25, low-sodium Communion will begin at 12:45, and sugar-free Communion will begin at 1:05."

"To meet the ever-growing needs of our congregation, Communion will begin this morning at 11:45. Fat-free Communion will begin at 12:05, high-fiber Communion will begin at 12:25, low-sodium Communion will begin at 12:45, and sugar-free Communion will begin at 1:05."

"To meet the ever-growing needs of our congregation, Communion will begin this morning at 11:45. Fat-free Communion will begin at 12:05, high-fiber Communion will begin at 12:25, low-sodium Communion will begin at 12:45, and sugar-free Communion will begin at 1:05."

"It's a proven fact that exercise makes people more alert. That's why we do all that kneeling and standing before my sermon."

"It's a proven fact that exercise makes people more alert. That's why we do all that kneeling and standing before my sermon."

"It's a proven fact that exercise makes people more alert. That's why we do all that kneeling and standing before my sermon."

"We're eating at church tonight. It's one of those pot gut dinners."

"We're eating at church tonight. It's one of those pot gut dinners."

"We're eating at church tonight. It's one of those pot gut dinners."

"The Lord caused me to lie down in green pastures once,
and I got in big trouble for getting grass stains on my good clothes."

"The Lord caused me to lie down in green pastures once,
and I got in big trouble for getting grass stains on my good clothes."

"The Lord caused me to lie down in green pastures once,
and I got in big trouble for getting grass stains on my good clothes."

"We banned the throwing of rice at weddings
right after Mildred Flotburn beaned her
new son-in-law with a full box of Uncle Ben's."

"We banned the throwing of rice at weddings
right after Mildred Flotburn beaned her
new son-in-law with a full box of Uncle Ben's."

"We banned the throwing of rice at weddings
right after Mildred Flotburn beaned her
new son-in-law with a full box of Uncle Ben's."

"NOW THAT WE'VE EACH HAD A CHANCE TO RESTATE THE
SAME POINT OF VIEW 40 TIMES OVER, I THINK WE CAN
COMFORTABLY MOVE ON TO THE NEXT TOPIC."

"NOW THAT WE'VE EACH HAD A CHANCE TO RESTATE THE
SAME POINT OF VIEW 40 TIMES OVER, I THINK WE CAN
COMFORTABLY MOVE ON TO THE NEXT TOPIC."

"NOW THAT WE'VE EACH HAD A CHANCE TO RESTATE THE
SAME POINT OF VIEW 40 TIMES OVER, I THINK WE CAN
COMFORTABLY MOVE ON TO THE NEXT TOPIC."

"I realize that humor is a vital part of many sermons, but are you sure it's wise to rewrite the Ten Commandments into *God's Top Ten List?*"

"I realize that humor is a vital part of many sermons, but are you sure it's wise to rewrite the Ten Commandments into *God's Top Ten List?*"

"I realize that humor is a vital part of many sermons, but are you sure it's wise to rewrite the Ten Commandments into *God's Top Ten List?*"

"Do you have to wear those sleeves because your muscles are really big?"

"Do you have to wear those sleeves because your muscles are really big?"

"Do you have to wear those sleeves because your muscles are really big?"

"THE REST OF THE BELL CHOIR IS OUT WITH THE FLU."

"THE REST OF THE BELL CHOIR IS OUT WITH THE FLU."

"THE REST OF THE BELL CHOIR IS OUT WITH THE FLU."

"WHAT'S THIS RUMOR I HEAR ABOUT SOME OF YOU SKIPPING MY SUNDAY SCHOOL CLASS?"

"WHAT'S THIS RUMOR I HEAR ABOUT SOME OF YOU SKIPPING MY SUNDAY SCHOOL CLASS?"

"WHAT'S THIS RUMOR I HEAR ABOUT SOME OF YOU SKIPPING MY SUNDAY SCHOOL CLASS?"

"WHAT'S THIS RUMOR I HEAR ABOUT SOME OF YOU SKIPPING MY SUNDAY SCHOOL CLASS?!"

"WHAT'S THIS RUMOR I HEAR ABOUT SOME OF YOU SKIPPING MY SUNDAY SCHOOL CLASS?!"

YEAH, THE PLUMBER SAYS IT'LL BE AT LEAST ANOTHER WEEK BEFORE THE SHOWER IS FIXED.

THE DOWNSIDE OF CARPOOLING.

YEAH, THE PLUMBER SAYS IT'LL BE AT LEAST ANOTHER WEEK BEFORE THE SHOWER IS FIXED.

THE DOWNSIDE OF CARPOOLING.

YEAH, THE PLUMBER SAYS IT'LL BE AT LEAST ANOTHER WEEK BEFORE THE SHOWER IS FIXED.

THE DOWNSIDE OF CARPOOLING.

"I HOPE THIS WON'T AFFECT MY GRADE."

"I HOPE THIS WON'T AFFECT MY GRADE."

"I HOPE THIS WON'T AFFECT MY GRADE."

"I HOPE THIS WON'T AFFECT MY GRADE"

"I HOPE THIS WON'T AFFECT MY GRADE"

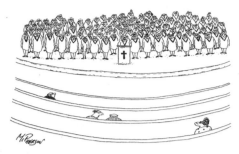

"IF YOU ASK ME, THEY GOT A LITTLE CARRIED AWAY WITH THE CHOIR MEMBERSHIP DRIVE."

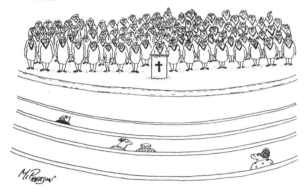

"IF YOU ASK ME, THEY GOT A LITTLE CARRIED AWAY WITH THE CHOIR MEMBERSHIP DRIVE."

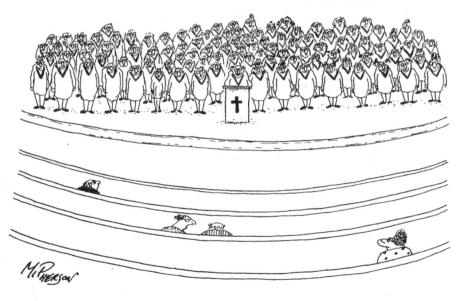

"IF YOU ASK ME, THEY GOT A LITTLE CARRIED AWAY WITH THE CHOIR MEMBERSHIP DRIVE."

"SORRY, SIR. I DIDN'T SEE THAT CATTLE CROSSING SIGN UNTIL IT WAS TOO LATE."

"SORRY, SIR. I DIDN'T SEE THAT CATTLE CROSSING SIGN UNTIL IT WAS TOO LATE."

"SORRY, SIR. I DIDN'T SEE THAT CATTLE CROSSING SIGN UNTIL IT WAS TOO LATE."

"SORRY, SIR, I DIDN'T SEE THAT CATTLE CROSSING
SIGN UNTIL IT WAS TOO LATE."

"SORRY, SIR, I DIDN'T SEE THAT CATTLE CROSSING
SIGN UNTIL IT WAS TOO LATE."

"SIR, I DIDN'T SEE THAT CATTLE CROSSING
SIGN UNTIL IT WAS TOO LATE."

"I have noticed that the congregation often pays more attention to the children's sermon than to the regular sermon. So today we're going to try something new..."

"I have noticed that the congregation often pays more attention to the children's sermon than to the regular sermon. So today we're going to try something new..."

"I have noticed that the congregation often pays more attention to the children's sermon than to the regular sermon. So today we're going to try something new..."

At Community Church potluck dinners, dental hygienist Jolene Gutburn was famous for her macaroni 'n' toothpaste casserole.

At Community Church potluck dinners, dental hygienist Jolene Gutburn was famous for her macaroni 'n' toothpaste casserole.

At Community Church potluck dinners, dental hygienist Jolene Gutburn was famous for her macaroni 'n' toothpaste casserole.

"We interviewed another new pastor for our church.
He had a voice like James Earl Jones, the oratory skills of Jack Kennedy,
the physical presence of Arnold Schwarzenegger, yet he was as patient
and gentle as Mister Rogers. We almost hired him, but Mrs. Duffy
didn't like his earring."

"We interviewed another new pastor for our church.
He had a voice like James Earl Jones, the oratory skills of Jack Kennedy,
the physical presence of Arnold Schwarzenegger, yet he was as patient
and gentle as Mister Rogers. We almost hired him, but Mrs. Duffy
didn't like his earring."

"We interviewed another new pastor for our church.
He had a voice like James Earl Jones, the oratory skills of Jack Kennedy,
the physical presence of Arnold Schwarzenegger, yet he was as patient
and gentle as Mister Rogers. We almost hired him, but Mrs. Duffy
didn't like his earring."

"Good morning. Today's sermon deals with modern
society's short attention span. The end. Amen."

"Good morning. Today's sermon deals with modern
society's short attention span. The end. Amen."

"Good morning. Today's sermon deals with modern
society's short attention span. The end. Amen."

PASTOR LIMKIN WAS EXTREMELY DISAPPOINTED WHEN
HE DISCOVERED THAT THE CONGREGATION'S SHOW OF
TOGETHERNESS WAS ACTUALLY CAUSED BY A BROKEN FURNACE.

PASTOR LIMKIN WAS EXTREMELY DISAPPOINTED WHEN
HE DISCOVERED THAT THE CONGREGATION'S SHOW OF
TOGETHERNESS WAS ACTUALLY CAUSED BY A BROKEN FURNACE.

PASTOR LIMKIN WAS EXTREMELY DISAPPOINTED WHEN
HE DISCOVERED THAT THE CONGREGATION'S SHOW OF
TOGETHERNESS WAS ACTUALLY CAUSED BY A BROKEN FURNACE.

THE BOARD MEMBERS KNEW THE IMPORTANCE OF UNWINDING
AFTER A HIGH-PRESSURE MEETING.

THE BOARD MEMBERS KNEW THE IMPORTANCE OF UNWINDING
AFTER A HIGH-PRESSURE MEETING.

THE BOARD MEMBERS KNEW THE IMPORTANCE OF UNWINDING
AFTER A HIGH-PRESSURE MEETING.

"OK, then it's settled. Next time we have the rock concert in the rec hall."

"OK, then it's settled. Next time we have the rock concert in the rec hall."

"OK, then it's settled. Next time we have the rock concert in the rec hall."

THE BANFORD VALLEY CHURCH STOOPS TO RAW COMMERCIALISM IN ITS ATTEMPT TO INCREASE ATTENDANCE.

THE BANFORD VALLEY CHURCH STOOPS TO RAW COMMERCIALISM IN ITS ATTEMPT TO INCREASE ATTENDANCE.

THE BANFORD VALLEY CHURCH STOOPS TO RAW COMMERCIALISM IN ITS ATTEMPT TO INCREASE ATTENDANCE.

" Boy, you can't smoke anywhere these days! "

James Cook

PORTLOCK

"I was fleeing sin. 1 Timothy 6:11."

" Boy, you can't smoke anywhere these days! "

James Cook

PORTLOCK

"I was fleeing sin. 1 Timothy 6:11."

" Boy, you can't smoke anywhere these days! "

James Cook

PORTLOCK

"I was fleeing sin. 1 Timothy 6:11."

AFTER THE SLIDE PROJECTOR BROKE, PASTOR SPACKLEY'S
VISUAL PRESENTATIONS TO THE BOARD TOOK A DRASTIC TURN FOR THE WORSE.

AFTER THE SLIDE PROJECTOR BROKE, PASTOR SPACKLEY'S
VISUAL PRESENTATIONS TO THE BOARD TOOK A DRASTIC TURN FOR THE WORSE.

AFTER THE SLIDE PROJECTOR BROKE, PASTOR SPACKLEY'S
VISUAL PRESENTATIONS TO THE BOARD TOOK A DRASTIC TURN FOR THE WORSE.

"If Jesus already paid for my sins,
how come I gotta stand in the corner for being bad?"

"If Jesus already paid for my sins,
how come I gotta stand in the corner for being bad?"

"If Jesus already paid for my sins,
how come I gotta stand in the corner for being bad?"

"NO, WOMEN'S ROLE IN MINISTRY IS NOT
A BIG ISSUE AT OUR CHURCH EITHER."

"NO, WOMEN'S ROLE IN MINISTRY IS NOT
A BIG ISSUE AT OUR CHURCH EITHER."

"GREATER SENSITIVITY! THAT'S THE MAIN THING I'VE
LEARNED FROM THE MARRIAGE WORKSHOP.
HOW ABOUT YOU?"

"GREATER SENSITIVITY! THAT'S THE MAIN THING I'VE
LEARNED FROM THE MARRIAGE WORKSHOP.
HOW ABOUT YOU?"

"If you tithe 10% of your income to God and 10% to me,
that still leaves you 80% to squander on yourselves!"

"If you tithe 10% of your income to God and 10% to me,
that still leaves you 80% to squander on yourselves!"

"I think we have everything: paper plates, soda, cold cuts, chips, dips, candy, napkins, hot dogs, hamburgers...oops! I forgot to invite the youth group."

"I think we have everything: paper plates, soda, cold cuts, chips, dips, candy, napkins, hot dogs, hamburgers...oops! I forgot to invite the youth group."

"I think we have everything: paper plates, soda, cold cuts, chips, dips, candy, napkins, hot dogs, hamburgers...oops! I forgot to invite the youth group."

James Cook

YEA, THOUGH I WALK THROUGH THE VALLEY OF THE SHADOW OF DEBT...

James Cook

YEA, THOUGH I WALK THROUGH THE VALLEY OF THE SHADOW OF DEBT...

James Cook

YEA, THOUGH I WALK THROUGH THE VALLEY OF THE SHADOW OF DEBT...

"YES, BUT CAN HE HANDLE BOARD MEETINGS?"

"YES, BUT CAN HE HANDLE BOARD MEETINGS?"

"Can't we talk about something besides religion for a change?"

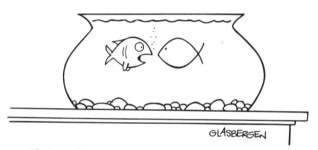

"Can't we talk about something besides religion for a change?"

AS SOON AS SHE BEGAN TO READ THE MINUTES OF THE LAST MEETING, THE BOARD MEMBERS KNEW THAT MRS. FELSTER WAS NOT GOING TO WORK OUT AS THE NEW SECRETARY.

AS SOON AS SHE BEGAN TO READ THE MINUTES OF THE LAST MEETING, THE BOARD MEMBERS KNEW THAT MRS. FELSTER WAS NOT GOING TO WORK OUT AS THE NEW SECRETARY.

"The church facilities are booked solid with civic organizations, special-interest meetings, and support groups. We'll have to find another place to hold our Sunday morning services!"

"The church facilities are booked solid with civic organizations, special-interest meetings, and support groups. We'll have to find another place to hold our Sunday morning services!"

"The church facilities are booked solid with civic organizations, special-interest meetings, and support groups. We'll have to find another place to hold our Sunday morning services!"

"Writing hymns is harder than I thought. I can't think of anything decent to rhyme with 'hallelujah' except 'glad I knew ya' and 'we'll tattoo ya'!"

"Writing hymns is harder than I thought. I can't think of anything decent to rhyme with 'hallelujah' except 'glad I knew ya' and 'we'll tattoo ya'!"

"Writing hymns is harder than I thought. I can't think of anything decent to rhyme with 'hallelujah' except 'glad I knew ya' and 'we'll tattoo ya'!"

"He says to pull over at the next oasis."

James Cook

"He says to pull over at the next oasis."

James Cook

"He says to pull over at the next oasis."

James Cook

"THEN IT'S SETTLED! WE PAINT THE SUNDAY SCHOOL ROOM BLUE!"

"THEN IT'S SETTLED! WE PAINT THE SUNDAY SCHOOL ROOM BLUE!"

"THEN IT'S SETTLED! WE PAINT THE SUNDAY SCHOOL ROOM BLUE!"

"PERSONALLY, I THINK THIS DONATION THING IS GETTING OUT OF HAND."

"PERSONALLY, I THINK THIS DONATION THING IS GETTING OUT OF HAND."

"PERSONALLY, I THINK THIS DONATION THING IS GETTING OUT OF HAND."

"I hate his clergier-than-thou attitude!"

"I hate his clergier-than-thou attitude!"

"I hate his clergier-than-thou attitude!"

"Our church youth group leader is a great guy
with a lot of energy, who really relates well
to kids. Either that, or he's just immature!"

**"Our church youth group leader is a great guy
with a lot of energy, who really relates well
to kids. Either that, or he's just immature!"**

**"Our church youth group leader is a great guy
with a lot of energy, who really relates well
to kids. Either that, or he's just immature!"**

"Today's service will be in 3-D."

"Today's service will be in 3-D."

"Today's service will be in 3-D."

"I'M THE CHAIRMAN PRO TEM OF THE BULLETIN INSERT SUBCOMMITTEE TO THE ADULT WORSHIP AND MUSIC EDUCATION BOARD ... WHAT'S YOUR SPIRITUAL GIFT?"

"I'M THE CHAIRMAN PRO TEM OF THE BULLETIN INSERT SUBCOMMITTEE TO THE ADULT WORSHIP AND MUSIC EDUCATION BOARD ... WHAT'S YOUR SPIRITUAL GIFT?"

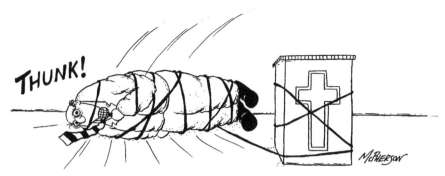

THIS INCIDENT PRETTY MUCH CONVINCED THE CONGREGATION TO PITCH IN AND GET PASTOR MENLEY A CORDLESS MICROPHONE.

"I'M THE CHAIRMAN PRO TEM OF THE BULLETIN INSERT SUBCOMMITTEE TO THE ADULT WORSHIP AND MUSIC EDUCATION BOARD ... WHAT'S YOUR SPIRITUAL GIFT?"

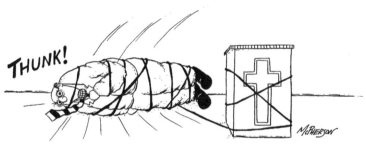

THIS INCIDENT PRETTY MUCH CONVINCED THE CONGREGATION TO PITCH IN AND GET PASTOR MENLEY A CORDLESS MICROPHONE.

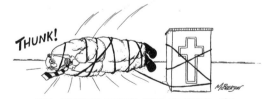

THIS INCIDENT PRETTY MUCH CONVINCED THE CONGREGATION TO PITCH IN AND GET PASTOR MENLEY A CORDLESS MICROPHONE.

"My client would also like his own private cloud. Will play nothing other than a pure golden harp. He also wants private trumpet lessons with Gabriel. And will wear only 100% cotton robes."

"My client would also like his own private cloud. Will play nothing other than a pure golden harp. He also wants private trumpet lessons with Gabriel. And will wear only 100% cotton robes."

"My client would also like his own private cloud. Will play nothing other than a pure golden harp. He also wants private trumpet lessons with Gabriel. And will wear only 100% cotton robes."

"We realize that our church camp isn't the fanciest place, but let's try to make the best of it! Whoever goes home with the most bug bites gets to come back next year for free!"

"We realize that our church camp isn't the fanciest place, but let's try to make the best of it! Whoever goes home with the most bug bites gets to come back next year for free!"

"We realize that our church camp isn't the fanciest place, but let's try to make the best of it! Whoever goes home with the most bug bites gets to come back next year for free!"

"That's the last time we let the youth group mow the lawn."

"That's the last time we let the youth group mow the lawn."

"That's the last time we let the youth group mow the lawn."

"RON, I'M YOUR LAB PARTNER. TRUST ME."

"RON, I'M YOUR LAB PARTNER. TRUST ME."

"RON, I'M YOUR LAB PARTNER. TRUST ME."

THE SPIRIT OF CHRISTMAS CAUSED A RARE DISPLAY OF GENEROSITY BY GYM TEACHER ART MANKOWSKI.

THE SPIRIT OF CHRISTMAS CAUSED A RARE DISPLAY OF GENEROSITY BY GYM TEACHER ART MANKOWSKI.

THE SPIRIT OF CHRISTMAS CAUSED A RARE DISPLAY OF GENEROSITY BY GYM TEACHER ART MANKOWSKI.

JONAH AND THE WHALE. THE LATER YEARS.

JONAH AND THE WHALE. THE LATER YEARS.

JONAH AND THE WHALE. THE LATER YEARS.

"I think I need a vacation. During my last baptism,
I almost married the baby to his older sister."

"I think I need a vacation. During my last baptism,
I almost married the baby to his older sister."

"I think I need a vacation. During my last baptism,
I almost married the baby to his older sister."

"OK, OK. The youth group can go to Disneyland."

"OK, OK. The youth group can go to Disneyland."

"OK, OK. The youth group can go to Disneyland."

"Could you pray with your eyes open, please?"

"Could you pray with your eyes open, please?"

"Could you pray with your eyes open, please?"

"They have a peculiar way of greeting first-time visitors."

"They have a peculiar way of greeting first-time visitors."

"They have a peculiar way of greeting first-time visitors."

"The pastor wanted me to bring up the subject of a higher housing allowance."

"The pastor wanted me to bring up the subject of a higher housing allowance."

"The pastor wanted me to bring up the subject of a higher housing allowance."

"JANITOR? NO! THAT'S OUR ASSOCIATE PASTOR."

"JANITOR? NO! THAT'S OUR ASSOCIATE PASTOR."

"JANITOR? NO! THAT'S OUR ASSOCIATE PASTOR."

"He says to let him out or it's the last beach party for the youth group."

"He says to let him out or it's the last beach party for the youth group."

"He says to let him out or it's the last beach party for the youth group."

"ALL I DID WAS HIT THE DELETE BUTTON!!"

"ALL I DID WAS HIT THE DELETE BUTTON!!"

"ALL I DID WAS HIT THE DELETE BUTTON!!"

PASTOR WAGMAN KNEW HE WAS ON A ROLL WHEN THE CONGREGATION STARTED DOING THE WAVE.

"WHY, YES, THESE ARE A FULL SET OF YOUR SERMON TAPES, PASTOR. JOHN USES THEM TO GET THE KIDS ASLEEP."

PASTOR WAGMAN KNEW HE WAS ON A ROLL WHEN THE CONGREGATION STARTED DOING THE WAVE.

"WHY, YES, THESE ARE A FULL SET OF YOUR SERMON TAPES, PASTOR. JOHN USES THEM TO GET THE KIDS ASLEEP."

PASTOR WAGMAN KNEW HE WAS ON A ROLL WHEN THE CONGREGATION STARTED DOING THE WAVE.

"WHY, YES, THESE ARE A FULL SET OF YOUR SERMON TAPES, PASTOR. JOHN USES THEM TO GET THE KIDS ASLEEP."

"ONCE AGAIN, I WANT TO STRESS THAT THE SERMON ILLUSTRATION I'VE JUST GIVEN IS PURELY FICTIONAL AND IS NOT BASED UPON ANYONE HERE IN THE CONGREGATION."

"ONCE AGAIN, I WANT TO STRESS THAT THE SERMON ILLUSTRATION I'VE JUST GIVEN IS PURELY FICTIONAL AND IS NOT BASED UPON ANYONE HERE IN THE CONGREGATION."

"ONCE AGAIN, I WANT TO STRESS THAT THE SERMON ILLUSTRATION I'VE JUST GIVEN IS PURELY FICTIONAL AND IS NOT BASED UPON ANYONE HERE IN THE CONGREGATION."

"Just a minute, there! Those haven't gone through committee!"

"Just a minute, there! Those haven't gone through committee!"

"Just a minute, there! Those haven't gone through committee!"

CHANGING THAT PESKY LIGHT IN THE SANCTUARY REQUIRED
A TEAM EFFORT FROM MEMBERS OF THE CONGREGATION.

UPON VISITING HIS FORMER CHURCH JUST THREE MONTHS AFTER
LEAVING, PASTOR BRUCE FERNLOCK DISCOVERS THAT HIS IMPACT
THERE WASN'T NEARLY AS PROFOUND AS HE HAD THOUGHT.

CHANGING THAT PESKY LIGHT IN THE SANCTUARY REQUIRED
A TEAM EFFORT FROM MEMBERS OF THE CONGREGATION.

UPON VISITING HIS FORMER CHURCH JUST THREE MONTHS AFTER
LEAVING, PASTOR BRUCE FERNLOCK DISCOVERS THAT HIS IMPACT
THERE WASN'T NEARLY AS PROFOUND AS HE HAD THOUGHT.

CHANGING THAT PESKY LIGHT IN THE SANCTUARY REQUIRED
A TEAM EFFORT FROM MEMBERS OF THE CONGREGATION.

UPON VISITING HIS FORMER CHURCH JUST THREE MONTHS AFTER
LEAVING, PASTOR BRUCE FERNLOCK DISCOVERS THAT HIS IMPACT
THERE WASN'T NEARLY AS PROFOUND AS HE HAD THOUGHT.

July 12th

Thanks to the summer slump,
Pastor Butterman was finally able
to try his hand at
intergenerational ministry.

JOHN LIKES TO ARRIVE EARLY
TO ASSURE HIMSELF A GOOD SEAT.

"WE'VE SAVED 10% ON OUR ELECTRICAL BILL BY HOOKING
THE WOMEN'S FITNESS CLASS UP TO A GENERATOR IN THE BASEMENT."

Thanks to the summer slump,
Pastor Butterman was finally able
to try his hand at
intergenerational ministry.

JOHN LIKES TO ARRIVE EARLY
TO ASSURE HIMSELF A GOOD SEAT.

"WE'VE SAVED 10% ON OUR ELECTRICAL BILL BY HOOKING
THE WOMEN'S FITNESS CLASS UP TO A GENERATOR IN THE BASEMENT."

"WE'VE SAVED 10% ON OUR ELECTRICAL BILL BY HOOKING
THE WOMEN'S FITNESS CLASS UP TO A GENERATOR IN THE BASEMENT."

"I REALLY DON'T KNOW WHO HE IS.
I SMILED AND SAID HI TO HIM IN THE HALLWAY,
AND HE'S BEEN THERE EVER SINCE."

"I REALLY DON'T KNOW WHO HE IS.
I SMILED AND SAID HI TO HIM IN THE HALLWAY,
AND HE'S BEEN THERE EVER SINCE."

"I REALLY DON'T KNOW WHO HE IS.
I SMILED AND SAID HI TO HIM IN THE HALLWAY,
AND HE'S BEEN THERE EVER SINCE."

Later, most folks would recall it as the last time they sang
"Just as I Am" in the early service.

Later, most folks would recall it as the last time they sang
"Just as I Am" in the early service.

Later, most folks would recall it as the last time they sang
"Just as I Am" in the early service.

"REMIND ME NEVER TO ASK THE YOUTH GROUP TO HELP FOLD THE CHURCH BULLETINS AGAIN."

"REMIND ME NEVER TO ASK THE YOUTH GROUP TO HELP FOLD THE CHURCH BULLETINS AGAIN."

"REMIND ME NEVER TO ASK THE YOUTH GROUP TO HELP FOLD THE CHURCH BULLETINS AGAIN."

"In Sunday school we learned how Jesus made a thousand meals from some bread and fish. My mom can do the same thing with Thanksgiving leftovers!"

"In Sunday school we learned how Jesus made a thousand meals from some bread and fish. My mom can do the same thing with Thanksgiving leftovers!"

"In Sunday school we learned how Jesus made a thousand meals from some bread and fish. My mom can do the same thing with Thanksgiving leftovers!"

Todd was glad the youth staff had read his request for a beach party, but wondered whether he needed to work on his penmanship.

Todd was glad the youth staff had read his request for a beach party, but wondered whether he needed to work on his penmanship.

Todd was glad the youth staff had read his request for a beach party, but wondered whether he needed to work on his penmanship.

"Two people signed up to scoop gunk out of the gutters, and 35 signed up as prayer support."

"Two people signed up to scoop gunk out of the gutters, and 35 signed up as prayer support."

"Two people signed up to scoop gunk out of the gutters, and 35 signed up as prayer support."

"LOOK, STAN, I'M SORRY ABOUT YOUR CAR. BUT, FRANKLY, I'M APPALLED THAT YOU, BEING A PASTOR, WOULD ALLOW YOURSELF TO BECOME UPSET OVER SOMETHING LIKE THIS."

"LOOK, STAN, I'M SORRY ABOUT YOUR CAR. BUT, FRANKLY, I'M APPALLED THAT YOU, BEING A PASTOR, WOULD ALLOW YOURSELF TO BECOME UPSET OVER SOMETHING LIKE THIS."

"LOOK, STAN, I'M SORRY ABOUT YOUR CAR. BUT, FRANKLY, I'M APPALLED THAT YOU, BEING A PASTOR, WOULD ALLOW YOURSELF TO BECOME UPSET OVER SOMETHING LIKE THIS."

"From now on, for the sake of political correctness, the original 12 disciples shall be known as Peter, Paul, Judas, Juan, Roberto, Big Eagle, Chang, Luigi, Helen, Mildred, Hannah, and Betty Ann."

"From now on, for the sake of political correctness, the original 12 disciples shall be known as Peter, Paul, Judas, Juan, Roberto, Big Eagle, Chang, Luigi, Helen, Mildred, Hannah, and Betty Ann."

"From now on, for the sake of political correctness, the original 12 disciples shall be known as Peter, Paul, Judas, Juan, Roberto, Big Eagle, Chang, Luigi, Helen, Mildred, Hannah, and Betty Ann."

"I have quite a lengthy list of announcements this morning. Please keep in mind that many of our brothers and sisters who are in the hospital may be out by the time I finish."

"I have quite a lengthy list of announcements this morning. Please keep in mind that many of our brothers and sisters who are in the hospital may be out by the time I finish."

"I have quite a lengthy list of announcements this morning. Please keep in mind that many of our brothers and sisters who are in the hospital may be out by the time I finish."

IT WASN'T HARD TO TELL THAT THESE WERE THE FIRST VISITORS ERWIN VALLEY CHURCH HAD HAD IN SEVEN YEARS.

IT WASN'T HARD TO TELL THAT THESE WERE THE FIRST VISITORS ERWIN VALLEY CHURCH HAD HAD IN SEVEN YEARS.

IT WASN'T HARD TO TELL THAT THESE WERE THE FIRST VISITORS ERWIN VALLEY CHURCH HAD HAD IN SEVEN YEARS.

"Clarence was committed to long-term youth ministry."

"Clarence was committed to long-term youth ministry."

"We're incompatible! I say 'ay-men' and she says 'ah-men'!"

"We're incompatible! I say 'ay-men' and she says 'ah-men'!"

GREAT MOMENTS IN HISTORY:
"BECAUSE WE'VE ALWAYS DONE IT THIS WAY! THAT'S
WHY!" ... IS SAID FOR THE FIRST TIME IN A CHURCH
BOARD MEETING.

GREAT MOMENTS IN HISTORY:
"BECAUSE WE'VE ALWAYS DONE IT THIS WAY! THAT'S
WHY!" ... IS SAID FOR THE FIRST TIME IN A CHURCH
BOARD MEETING.

GREAT MOMENTS IN HISTORY:
"BECAUSE WE'VE ALWAYS DONE IT THIS WAY! THAT'S
WHY!" ... IS SAID FOR THE FIRST TIME IN A CHURCH
BOARD MEETING.

For some reason, Daniel began to feel uneasy.

For some reason, Daniel began to feel uneasy.

For some reason, Daniel began to feel uneasy.

That humiliating moment when you realize that the bulletin said to sing verses 1, 2, and 3, but not 4.

That humiliating moment when you realize that the bulletin said to sing verses 1, 2, and 3, but not 4.

That humiliating moment when you realize that the bulletin said to sing verses 1, 2, and 3, but not 4.

"I think they're missing the whole point."

"I think they're missing the whole point."

"I think they're missing the whole point."

"I THINK WHAT MRS. NITWHIPPLE IS TRYING TO SAY IS
THAT WE NEED HELP WITH THE SIXTH-GRADERS THIS MORNING."

"I THINK WHAT MRS. NITWHIPPLE IS TRYING TO SAY IS
THAT WE NEED HELP WITH THE SIXTH-GRADERS THIS MORNING."

"I THINK WHAT MRS. NITWHIPPLE IS TRYING TO SAY IS
THAT WE NEED HELP WITH THE SIXTH-GRADERS THIS MORNING."

"I THINK IT'S TIME WE ALL PITCHED IN AND BOUGHT
THE CHOIR SOME CLASSIER-LOOKING ROBES."

"I THINK IT'S TIME WE ALL PITCHED IN AND BOUGHT
THE CHOIR SOME CLASSIER-LOOKING ROBES."

"I THINK IT'S TIME WE ALL PITCHED IN AND BOUGHT
THE CHOIR SOME CLASSIER-LOOKING ROBES."

"MY DOG ATE IT."

"MY DOG ATE IT."

"MY DOG ATE IT."

Parking Lot Resurfacing Committee members were the first to suspect Pastor Fred had become "amen dependent."

Parking Lot Resurfacing Committee members were the first to suspect Pastor Fred had become "amen dependent."

Parking Lot Resurfacing Committee members were the first to suspect Pastor Fred had become "amen dependent."

Audrey felt a little awkward, not being familiar with the liturgy.

Audrey felt a little awkward, not being familiar with the liturgy.

"You're all turning into mature, responsible young people, which is playing havoc with our belching contests."

Audrey felt a little awkward, not being familiar with the liturgy.

"You're all turning into mature, responsible young people, which is playing havoc with our belching contests."

"You're all turning into mature, responsible young people, which is playing havoc with our belching contests."

"He must be from another denomination."

James Cook

"He must be from another denomination."

James Cook

NEXT
5 MILES

James Cook

NEXT
5 MILES

James Cook

"I think our congregation has been watching too much football on TV."

"I think our congregation has been watching too much football on TV."

"OUR DONATIONS HAVE DOUBLED SINCE WE HAD THAT THING INSTALLED!"

"OUR DONATIONS HAVE DOUBLED SINCE WE HAD THAT THING INSTALLED!"

"OUR DONATIONS HAVE DOUBLED SINCE WE HAD THAT THING INSTALLED!"

NEWCOMERS TO TWINDLE VALLEY CHURCH QUICKLY SENSED THAT THIS WAS A CONGREGATION WITH TWO VERY DISTINCT FACTIONS.

NEWCOMERS TO TWINDLE VALLEY CHURCH QUICKLY SENSED THAT THIS WAS A CONGREGATION WITH TWO VERY DISTINCT FACTIONS.

NEWCOMERS TO TWINDLE VALLEY CHURCH QUICKLY SENSED THAT THIS WAS A CONGREGATION WITH TWO VERY DISTINCT FACTIONS.

THURSTON HIGH COULDN'T AFFORD
A TRAMPOLINE.

THURSTON HIGH COULDN'T AFFORD
A TRAMPOLINE.

THURSTON HIGH COULDN'T AFFORD
A TRAMPOLINE.

"WHAT DO YOU THINK, HONEY?
IS THAT ILLUSTRATION TOO INTENSE?"

"WHAT DO YOU THINK, HONEY?
IS THAT ILLUSTRATION TOO INTENSE?"

"WHAT DO YOU THINK, HONEY?
IS THAT ILLUSTRATION TOO INTENSE?"

James Cook

"ONLY TWO, I KEEP TELLIN' YA, ONLY TWO!"

James Cook

"ONLY TWO, I KEEP TELLIN' YA, ONLY TWO!"

James Cook

"ONLY TWO, I KEEP TELLIN' YA, ONLY TWO!"

"WELL, AT LAST WE HAVE A VOLUNTEER TO DO THE ORAL REPORT ON OSMOSIS."

"WELL, AT LAST WE HAVE A VOLUNTEER TO DO THE ORAL REPORT ON OSMOSIS."

"WELL, AT LAST WE HAVE A VOLUNTEER TO DO THE ORAL REPORT ON OSMOSIS."

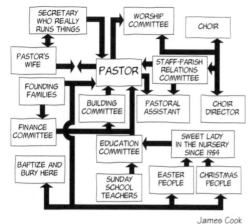

James Cook

STELLA KNEW THE IMPORTANCE OF BEING DISCREET
WHEN MAKING PERSONAL PHONE CALLS.

STELLA KNEW THE IMPORTANCE OF BEING DISCREET
WHEN MAKING PERSONAL PHONE CALLS.

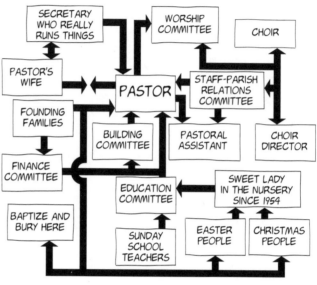

James Cook

"OOOO! ... I REALLY FELT **CONVICTED** BY
YOUR SERMON TODAY, CHAPLAIN."

"Do you have mustard seed?"

"MOST OF US ARE COMMITTED TO FURTHERING GOD'S KINGDOM, BUT WE'RE NOT QUITE SURE WHAT HAWKINS IS COMMITTED TO FURTHERING."

"MOST OF US ARE COMMITTED TO FURTHERING GOD'S KINGDOM, BUT WE'RE NOT QUITE SURE WHAT HAWKINS IS COMMITTED TO FURTHERING."

"The priest is here to help you. The lady wants your apartment."

"Do you have mustard seed?"

"The priest is here to help you. The lady wants your apartment."

YEARS OF PEOPLE STICKING THEIR GUM
UNDER DESKS WERE STARTING TO TAKE
THEIR TOLL.

"Remember, this is a *church* picnic—so always say 'amen' after you burp!"

"Remember, this is a *church* picnic—so always say 'amen' after you burp!"

YEARS OF PEOPLE STICKING THEIR GUM
UNDER DESKS WERE STARTING TO TAKE
THEIR TOLL.

"All I ask is to be inspired and home by kickoff time."

"All I ask is to be inspired and home by kickoff time."

SUBJECT GUIDE